GLAM! AN EYEWITNESS ACCOUNT
MICK ROCK
FOREWORD BY DAVID BOWIE

I DON'T GO INTO A SESSION INTENDING TO MAKE ANY KIND
HOW TO EXPLORE THE UNIQUE ENIGMA OF THE SITUATION.
AS IT IS ABOUT REVEALING. THE RESOLUTION LIES IN THE
MAGIC MOMENT.

MICK ROCK 1981

I LOVE GIRLS. THEY'RE SMASHIN'.
THEY'RE AS GOOD AS BLOKES.
DAVID BOWIE 1972

Ziggy Stardust fans
UK 1973

ANYTHING CAN BE SEX. GETTING OFF IS SEX. GETTING TO AN AUDIENCE IS SEX. LOOKING IS SEX. YOUR BODY IS A FRAMEWORK WITH INFINITE POSSIBILITIES. IT'S JUST A QUESTION OF TAPPING ONE OF THEM.

LOU REED 1975

I SAW THE DULL YELLOW EYE OF THE CREATURE OPEN; IT BREATHED HARD, AND A CONVULSIVE MOTION AGITATED ITS LIMBS.

MARY SHELLEY, *FRANKENSTEIN*, 1818

Lindsay Kemp & Troupe
London 1974

Rocky Horror Picture Show
Bray Studios, Autumn 1974

FOREWORD

Of course, when it comes down to it, it was all very amusing. At the time it was funny, then, a few years later it became sort of serious looking and a bit foreboding. Lots of Post-Modernist juxtapositions and elements substituting as subversive, though 'significant' ciphers, that kind of twaddle. Now? Well, now it's just funny again, albeit with a certain clout.

One overriding and mischievous satisfaction that I still derive immense pleasure from is remembering how many hod-carrying brickies were encouraged to put on lurex tights and mince up and down the high street, having been assured by know-it-alls like me, that a smidgen of blusher really attracted the birds. This, of course, was true. And has always been since woad.

However, for the likes of Roxy Music and myself, mascara was merely the conveyance by which great globs of non-rock flotsam and jetsam were to be delivered. Japanese kabuki, Dada, Dietrich and Leni Riefenstahl, Piaf and Futurism, and above all, 'elegant gloom' as author Barney Hoskyns has put it. Not for us the couple of pints in the backroom bar after the gig. We were wondering where to lay our hands on absinthe, puzzling through McCluen, the big questions: greasepaint or pancake? Climbing the heights of what we felt was much-needed pretension, we were above common-or-garden chat-up lines to dodgy slappers. We craved the rarefied stratosphere from whence we dropped really heavy names: Burroughs, Brecht and Baudelaire tumbled meaninglessly over Warhol and Wittgenstein in a blur of de- and re-constructed Pop.

Let me back pedal for a second. Pretension, or the 'School of Pretension' as I pretentiously dubbed Eno and myself later in 1978, was a quick fix category for it all. By 1970 the knock-on effect of The Dice Man, Warhol's culture flattening and the breakdances of Derrida and Foucault had substantially changed the notion of 'the absolute', of reality. It was no longer possible to take the history of things as stage-managed by the media and the educational system seriously. Everything we knew was wrong. Burroughs, being the John the Baptist of Post-Modernism, had proselytized over this point for years. Free at last or, if you like, at sea without a paddle, we were giving permission to ourselves to reinvent culture the way we wanted it. With great big shoes.

Well, all right, if you insist. We couldn't have pounced without Marc Bolan. The little imp opened the door. What was so great, however, was that we knew he hadn't got it quite right. Sort of Glam 1.0. We were straining in the wings with versions 1.01 and 1.02, while Marc was still struggling with satin. But boy, he really rocked. He did, y'know?

Annoyingly, of course, Americans often make overly steep territorial claims for the U.S. as the spawning ground for this brief movement, as they usually do with Punk and television. Yes, we loved American underground music and John Rechy's City of Night but we really did have our own drag queens and drugs in London, thank you very much. We also had A Clockwork Orange, Lindsay Kemp, Berlin and Fritz Lang, George Orwell and Nietzsche, Yamamoto Kansai (one hundred percent responsible for the Ziggy haircut and colour, by the by), Mishima's gay army and Colin Wilson to draw upon. (I could list *ad nauseam*, and have been known to do so, as the ingredients for high-glam were dizzyingly disparate). And if I read one more self-aggrandizing denizen of the Big Apple screaming blue murder over the issue of who established the shaved eyebrow first, well gosh, I'll just hurl. But the truth is, as wonderful as the New York Dolls were, and they were, they were just The Stones in lamé. The Americans at heart are a pure and noble people. Things to them are in black and white. It's either 'rawk' or it's not. We Brits putter around in the grey area. In our minds it's 'a little bit rock, a little bit snigger'.

British Glam Rock never made an impact on Middle America to any extent. Before and aft, we were bookended by Alice and Kiss, butch 'manly' glam with lots of guillotines and fireworks, muscle and metal. No mistaking the sexual bent of those fellas. 'Nothing ambiguous about our boys'. That's the only way Ohio could accept lipstick on males. So we Limeys all swanned off sniffily to the wings where we did make an impression. For a brief moment or two, we ruled in New York and Los Angeles.

Have a look at all of these jolly pictures. Boys having fun, with some girls too. Next week I'll be showing you how to turn all those earrings into a perfectly serviceable chain with which you can anchor yourself for the oncoming tremors of 1975. All you'll need will be a snotty nose, an abused Ziggy haircut and an ability to pronounce 'anarchy'. Me? I'll be fucking off to Berlin, thanks.

David Bowie
New York City, February 2001

David Bowie
Beckenham, March 1972

David Bowie and Mick Rock
Chateau D'Herouville
Paris 1973

There's an art to looking back - how to celebrate the past without being entrapped by it. Photographs provide the great physical link. Look how young, outrageous and fabulous we all were. Look how dead and decayed are some. Look how wise have become the survivors, soberly acknowledging that indeed only the chosen die young. It's an old tale of experiments in mind, flesh and imagination; of selective sin and occasional redemption.

The true art of being young is knowing how to defy gravity and upset as many people as possible while doing it. How to penetrate the great secrets of the universe and damn the torpedoes. How to stir the demons of our destiny...

If this is starting to sound like a confession, then maybe it is. Having stared my own mortality in its cruel eye some four years ago, and having so to speak been reborn (but not born again), I know that the flesh and its organs are as fragile as they are robust, and that mind is a deviant and devastating mistress. In truth I'm thrilled to still be here. *God bless us, everyone.*

As with all cultural movements great and small, Glam - like its unruly younger sibling Punk - was founded on unique and radical personae whose sensibilities so perfectly reflected and inflected the times they inhabited. These were the individuals I was drawn to. My ambition was not to be a great photographer (though that certainly would have been a worthy stance). It was a lust to embrace anything that startled or energised me. This was the road down which my instinct for the colourful and decadent led me. And in the process I captured moments in time that still resonate today. I certainly wasn't trying to consciously document or define. I just needed to prime my nervous system on the sharpest edges of my time.

Timing, as we all must conclude, is just about everything - in life, relationships, music, art, fashion and most of all in photography. The artful snap of the shutter. The sense that THIS frame will tell the whole fabulous story - seized in one single, sharp instant. Frozen forever. What a privilege. Not better than sex, but tapped from the same sizzling source. Rock this one, Socrates. Let the picture open its silver nitrate throat and shriek. Like an electric guitar. Delight in the power to enslave the glorious moment. And never second guess...

A camera is a wonderful ally. It requires minimal maintenance and provides entry to a world of endless imagery. Follow the frame, says I. Gnaw on the never-ending present. Believe in everything. Throw out all the rules and caress the tiniest twitch, the loneliest thrill, the blessed image. A life on the metaphysical lam... now that feels good.

So, by early 1972, Gay and Feminist cultures were on the rise and I had already acquired an occasional, deliciously illicit taste for eyeliner, rouge and lipgloss. The planets had found a

FRANKLY, READING ABOUT ROCK BORES ME STIFF.
DAVID BOWIE 1973

new alignment and were showing off. It was a time of unique alliances and ancient resonances... from the breast of the beast sweet lactations, from the heart of darkness androgyny run wild...

Glitter was abroad, chiefly manifested in the elfin figure of Marc Bolan with T. Rex, who had dominated the UK singles chart for the previous twelve months. Now I wasn't that taken with Bolan's music - few people over eighteen were. It was kiddie stuff. In truth, I have long since revised that opinion. But that was then. My prime musical obsession was the little-known, Andy Warhol-sponsored, cult New York group The Velvet Underground (who by now had been defunct for some eighteen months). From *I'll Be Your Mirror* to *Sister Ray* to *Sweet Jane*, who needed T. Rex? But, of course, as the years thundered on, I came to understand that if Bowie was Glam's Messiah, then Bolan was its John the Baptist...

When I first met David Bowie in early 1972, he was best known, if at all, for wearing a dress on an album jacket (the original cover of *The Man Who Sold the World*). Nobody I knew was familiar with his work. At the time, among other related activities, I was doing the occasional photo-interview for a number of magazines. Nothing too substantial. A page here, a half-page there. My most significant cultural relationship had been with Syd Barrett, a friend since my student days before I ever knew how to aim a lens. Then on the edge of my

dreamscape an alien blip... Blink once and you're gone, blink thrice and you're free...

I had recently obsessed over a cast-off promo copy of *Hunky Dory*, an album that had made no dent on English pop consciousness. To my ears, it was the most intriguing music since The Velvets, and then there was that face on the cover, couldn't tell if it was a boy or a girl... Is there Life on Mars? That was always the question. The answer is unimportant. The question was everything...

So I sought David out, which wasn't difficult at this point, since he was hungry for any kind of publicity. At the first show I witnessed there were three or four hundred people so he already had a small, but energised, following. And I was totally impressed. There was an unexpected passion and refinement to his delivery. It was clear that in his mind he was performing for a much larger audience. He was very distinctive, very different, and strangely colourful. He soon informed me that he had learned mostly about theatrical presentation from Lindsay Kemp, who was himself barely known outside esoteric circles at the time: how catching the eye was the key. First you seduce the retina, then you subvert the other senses. The first rule of Glam. So I interviewed him at length and soaked up his uniqueness with my lens. He was very enthusiastic, totally charming and very informed. Clearly a man on a mission: with Ziggy Stardust, alter ego, his chosen means. In time I came to realise how prescient he was. We had many tastes in common, from Syd Barrett to the Velvet Underground, Baudelaire to Cocteau, A Clockwork Orange to 2001.

As Ziggy rose and stoked the flames of the fabulously erupting Glam scene, so in his wake he dragged many other artists out of the twilight zone and onto the map, including Lou Reed, Iggy Pop, Mott the Hoople, Lindsay Kemp, Mick Ronson, and to a more modest degree, myself. I had acquired the keys to the kingdom (pictures of Ziggy) and I never looked back. The timing and aesthetic of my relationship with David gave me a unique cachet. I couldn't have scripted it better. Fame was the flame. Rock'n'Roll was the game. Glam was the vehicle. I was an instant believer, an intuitive instrument in the propagation of image. I was in a perfect place at a perfect moment and I didn't even know it, but I pursued it with all the focus of passionate ignorance.

I seemed to be everywhere. And I was. In truth there were very few hip photographers in those delightful days - and none had the appetite for mascara that I did. Those were very different times in the media. The rise of Punk a few years after generated a new posse of superhip shutterbugs. But that was later. Mostly, I was the only lensman present at the key moments. I was not an outsider looking in. This was my scene. I lived it. I had close friendships with many of my subjects. *All the Young*

Dudes... Well, we were all still very young in those steamy days of satin and tat.

Now the only primary figure I didn't photograph was Marc Bolan. And therein lies a tale or two. I did meet him at parties and we did discuss photosessions. But by then his star was in serious decline and he was desperate and unhappy and über-stoned. David and he had some kind of falling out just before the rise of Ziggy and they weren't talking. My relationship with David and my relative disinterest in Marc's music precluded any serious rapport. Later Marc and David rekindled their friend- ship but Marc was never able to turn up the media volume again, and then he died so tragically...

The rockers were the most obvious manifestations of the Glam sensibility, and the individuals who most readily understood its publicity value. Even more seasoned performers such as Mick Jagger, Elton John and Rod Stewart adapted to the allure of Glam when it was in full throttle. But it was David, Lou, Iggy and, a little later, Roxy Music, Freddie Mercury and Queen who were the significant icons. They were the sensibility purveyors. They changed the way most inquisitive individuals of that time felt, thought, dressed and lived. And they are also the ones who have cast the longest shadows, even into this new millennium. At the time, they seemed to be star-crazed irrationals run amok. Now I was a very impressionable young man. If I was energised by an artist or

Lou Reed
London 1974

his work or an event, I would pursue it like a fiend. My interest was never about fame, success or money. In fact, such rewards were in extremely short supply for photographers, in those very different times. I wasn't looking to acquire anything (except images and impressions). I wanted to absorb, revel in and celebrate a bright, magical time when everything I lensed sparkled like firefly.

I have often been asked in the years in between about my favourite photo subjects, my most memorable sessions, my most prized frames. And while such questions have to be asked, in truth, I have affection for anyone who has ever graced my lens. Well, maybe a little more for some than for others. But that's for you to guess and me to assess.

However, it would be reasonable to assert that the subjects of this humble tome, splattered with the glitter and blood of my long-lost youth, have provided the greatest resonance for my rock'n'roll eye. This was a time when I partook of my most enduring lessons in the alchemy of image-making and the mystery of its durability.

Certainly Glam was about make-up, mirrors and androgyny. It was narcissistic, obsessive, decadent and subversive. It was bohemian, but also strangely futuristic. It was Oscar Wilde meets A Clockwork Orange. It was a mutant bastard offspring of Glitter. But while Glitter was sparkling distraction,

Glam was anarchy in drag. It was sexy, glamorous, on the edge. It was the moment Hippie finally died. It was absolutely Rock'n'Roll. But it was also fashion, art, theatre, lifestyle. It was gay, straight, multisexual. It was totally titillating and absolutely naughty. Everybody held hands with everybody, kissed everybody, went home with everybody. It was an age of accelerated discovery, when all the kinks of sexual yearning were flushed out. It was absolutely self-indulgent and it was ridiculously camp. It was a time we thought would never end. A time so long ago now it seems like a dream. But it wasn't, and I have the pictures to prove it. Long live the angels of our destiny...

Mick Rock
New York City, January 2001

THERE ARE TIMES IN SESSIONS WHEN I'M A LIVE WIRE. THERE'S A MOMENT WHEN MY SUBJECT WILL BECOME COMPLETELY GLUED TO THE END OF MY LENS AND I CAN LITERALLY FEEL THEM TWITCHING.

IT'S A SHARP, CLEAR SENSATION. I DON'T HAVE TO SEE THEM ANYMORE BECAUSE I'M TOTALLY IDENTIFIED WITH THEM.

Mick Rock
London 1974
Photo by Lou Reed

I SMELL PICTURES MORE THAN I SEE
THEM. AND I HEAR PICTURES MORE THAN
I SMELL THEM. IT'S VERY HABIT FORMING.

MICK ROCK 1979

Iggy Pop
Fulham Road rehearsal studios.
London, Summer 1974

FREDDIE WAS ALWAYS A STAR. I REMEMBER HIM PENNILESS
YEARS AGO COMING ROUND TO MINE TO BUM A NIGHT'S
SLEEP ON THE FLOOR AND HE'D ALWAYS ACT LIKE HE WAS
DOING YOU A FAVOUR.

ROGER TAYLOR 1974

Freddie Mercury
Holland Road
London, Summer 1974

THAT'S ALL I WANTED TO DO AS A KID. PLAY A GUITAR PROPERLY AND JUMP AROUND.
BUT TOO MANY PEOPLE GOT IN THE WAY. IT'S ALWAYS BEEN TOO SLOW FOR ME. PLAYING. THE
PACE OF THINGS. I MEAN, I'M A FAST SPRINTER. THE TROUBLE WAS AFTER PLAYING IN THE
GROUP FOR A FEW MONTHS, I COULDN'T REACH THAT POINT ANY MORE.

SYD BARRETT 1971

Syd Barrett
Earl's Court.
London, Summer 1969

I'M SORRY I CAN'T SPEAK VERY COHERENTLY.
IT'S RATHER DIFFICULT TO THINK OF ANYONE BEING
REALLY INTERESTED IN ME. BUT YOU KNOW, MAN,
I'M TOTALLY TOGETHER. I DON'T THINK I'M EASY TO
TALK ABOUT. I'VE GOT A VERY IRREGULAR HEAD.
AND I'M NOT ANYTHING THAT YOU THINK I AM.

SYD BARRETT 1971

I FIRST PHOTOGRAPHED HIM IN 1969 AT THE TIME OF THE MADCAP LAUGHS. I HAD ACQUIRED A 28MM LENS FOR MY BATTERED SECOND-HAND PENTAX THE DAY BEFORE. SYD WAS MY FIRST EXPERIMENT WITH IT. HE WAS VERY UNHAPPY AND WITHDRAWN AND HAD LEFT PINK FLOYD. BUT HE ALLOWED ME TO CONNECT WITH HIS RAGING, BEAUTIFUL LUMINOSITY. THAT AFTERNOON WAS THE FIRST TIME I WAS TRULY CHARGED WITH THE ALCHEMICAL POWER OF CAMERA AND FILM.

SYD WAS CURIOUS TO SEE THE RESULTS, BUT HE DIDN'T WANT ANY PRINTS FOR HIMSELF. I FELT HE WAS ALMOST FRIGHTENED BY THE POWER OF HIS OWN IMAGE. THE GIRL IN THE PHOTO WAS KNOWN AS IGGY THE ESKIMO. SHE WAS LIVING WITH SYD AT THE TIME. I DON'T THINK HE KNEW HER REAL NAME. I NEVER DID FIND OUT WHAT HAPPENED TO HER.

MICK ROCK 1979

Syd on his Buick
Syd never drove the car. Eventually, it was towed away by local authorities.
Earl's Court, London 1969

ROCK STARS HAVE TAKEN OVER FROM THE
FALSE PROPHETS OF JESUS' TIME, SPREADING A
PHONEY RELIGION AND GETTIN' PAID FOR IT.
DAVID BOWIE 1973

David Bowie
Earl's Court, May 1973

Beckenham, April 1972

WHAT DO THEY WANT OF ME? THAT'S THE JOKE OF IT. BUT
CLOWNS. AND THIS IS THE MOST ENJOYABLE WAY I KNOW C
UPHOLSTERY? NO - THERE'S REALLY NOTHING ELSE. I'LL 'AV
DON'T KNOW WHAT THERE'LL BE LEFT TO DO.

DAVID BOWIE 1973

AGAIN PEOPLE NEED FIGURES LIKE ME, THE
AKING A LIVING. WHAT ELSE WOULD I DO?
DIE BY THE TIME I'M THIRTY, 'CAUSE I

IT WAS THIS INFAMOUS SHOT THAT DID IT.
OXFORD HALL, JUNE 1972. FULL HOUSE. I WAS A
MARKED MAN AFTER THAT. THE MAN WHO
SHOT ZIGGY STARDUST.
AT DAVID'S REQUEST, I STAYED UP LATE THAT
NIGHT TO PROCESS THE FILM AND MAKE PRINTS.
AT NOON THE NEXT DAY I MET DAVID AT HIS
MANAGEMENT OFFICES NEAR OXFORD CIRCUS.
WE PINNED THIS SHOT TO THE BULLETIN BOARD.
"THAT'LL GET THEM AT IT," HE BEAMED.
HE PERSUADED HIS MANAGER TO BUY A FULL
PAGE IN MELODY MAKER. WE COULD JUST MAKE
THE DEADLINE. HE WROTE A MESSAGE TO HIS
FANS ALONG THE SIDE OF THE PRINT, "HEY, HEY,
I JUST CAN'T THANK YOU ENUFF. LOVE ZIGGY."
THE PHOTOGRAPH WAS AN INDELIBLE IMAGE. IT
EXCITED EVERYONE AND OPENED A VERY SPECIAL
DOOR FOR ME... I DIDN'T LOOK BACK FOR
TWENTY YEARS.

MICK ROCK 1983

David Bowie and Mick Ronson
Oxford Town Hall.
June 1972

THEY WERE PROBABLY THE
BEST TIMES, EARLY ON,
WHEN DAVID DECIDED TO
CALL US 'THE SPIDERS FROM
MARS'. BECAUSE EVERY-
THING WAS NEW AND
DIFFERENT. AND WHEN IT
STARTED TO HAPPEN, IT
HAPPENED SO FAST THERE
WAS NO TIME TO THINK OR
WORRY ABOUT ANYTHING.
THEN IT ALL GOT SO UNREAL,
AND DAVE FOUND IT HARD
TO CONTROL.

MICK RONSON 1975

Ziggy and the Spiders from Mars
'Jean Genie' promo film.
San Francisco, November 1972

I NEVER HAD A TALENT FOR DRAWING BUT I DO THINK IN TE
ALWAYS SEEN MY LIFE AS BEING SOME KIND OF MOVIE. PEO
SIMILAR TO THE MOVIE, BLOW UP. IT'S NO JOKE, ACTUALLY.
FLOOR. I'VE DONE A LOT OF THAT IN MY TIME.

MICK ROCK 1986

David Bowie with Cyrinda Foxe
A bar in Beverly Hills. A frame in this session was used in a few US magazine ads for his new single 'Jean Genie.'
November 1972

I'M ONE OF THE WORLD'S ACTORS, IN THE BROADEST
SENSE OF THE WORD. I'M AN EXHIBITIONIST.
I LIKE SHOWING OFF. I'M A PEACOCK.
DAVID BOWIE 1973

MIME IS THE ART OF CONVEYING ONE'S FEELINGS
FABULOUSLY WITHOUT NOTICEABLY DOING ANYTHING.
IT ISN'T THE ART OF MOVEMENT. IT'S THE ART OF
SILENCE AND STILLNESS.

LINDSAY KEMP 1975

David Bowie
Lindsay Kemp designed the set.
His troupe provided choreographed
performance in support. This was the first
time Bowie presented a full-scale
theatrical setting for his performance.
Two nights at the Rainbow Theatre,
Finsbury Park, London, August 1972

I EXPERIENCED DAVID BOWIE ABOVE ALL AS A
PIECE OF LIVING ARTWORK, CONSTANTLY MODULATING
AND MUTATING LIKE A SERIES OF STARTLING REFLECTIONS
IN A CRACKED MIRROR. HE WAS FASCINATING: ZIGGY
STARDUST WAS A NEW BREED OF ROCK'N'ROLL
OPERATIVE, A ROGUE HITMAN WITH HIS OWN AGENDA,
A POST-MODERN HEARTTHROB WITH DESTINY ON HIS
MIND, A DREAMER OF DADA WITH GLITTER IN HIS SOUL.

HE WAS THE SCARLET PIMPERNEL IN FABULOUS
DRAG. HE WAS WHAT THE TIMES NEEDED AND A
WHOLE LOT MORE.

MICK ROCK 1986

Andrew Logan in Mick Rock's studio
Great Newport Street, London 1974

Angie Bowie
Beckenham, Summer 1973

Queen
'Queen II' photosession. The mirror
was provided by Freddie Mercury.
London 1974

Iggy Pop
Fulham Road rehearsal studio.
Summer 1974

Lou Reed
In his rented apartment, during the recording of 'Transformer'.
Wimbledon, Summer 1972

BOWIE MADE PEOPLE SO MUCH SEXIER. I MEAN, MEN IN MAKE-UP, AREN'T
THEY MUCH SEXIER? IT'S A PITY HE'S MADE WOMEN LOOK LIKE MALE IMPERSONATORS,
BUT HE HAS BROUGHT GLAMOUR TO THE STREETS.

LINDSAY KEMP 1974

Lindsay Kemp
Great Newport Street, Spring 1974

Lindsay with Mick Rock
*Party for West End production of
'Flowers' mime play.*
London 1974

Lindsay and David
Bush Theatre.
London 1973

MY DREAMS ARE VERY CLOSE TO MY REALITIES AND THEY ALSO PAY THE RENT.
LINDSAY KEMP 1974

THE MOVEMENT OR GESTURE FOR ME IS MERELY
THE EXQUISITE JOURNEY TO THE ATTITUDE, WHICH
IS THE STATE OF ECSTASY.

LINDSAY KEMP 1974

DAVID HAS A PERFECT FACE FOR MAKE-UP,
YOU SEE. HE HAS EVEN FEATURES, HIGH CHEEKBONES
AND A VERY GOOD MOUTH. I HAVE TO BE CAREFUL
THOUGH BECAUSE HIS SKIN IS VERY FINE AND SOME OF
THE BASE POWDERS I USE ARE VERY STRONG.
THEY CAN MAKE THE FACE QUITE SORE.

PIERRE LAROCHE 1974

Pierre Laroche making up Lindsay Kemp
For a performance of 'The Maids'.
Bush Theatre, London 1974

Pierre with David
'Life On Mars' promo film.
Summer 1973

Pierre - 'Glam make-up master'
*Worked on 'Aladdin Sane' and 'Pinups'
album covers with Bowie. Also designed
make-up for 'Rocky Horror Picture Show'.
Other clients included Marc Bolan
and Mick Jagger.*
London 1974

MY MOTHER SAW A LOT OF ACTORS IN SOUTH SHIELDS AND IT USED TO WORRY HER THAT THEY ONLY EVER HAD ONE PAIR OF SHOES. WHEN SHE TOOK ME TO THE LOCAL REP, SHE'D POINT OUT THAT WHETHER THEY WERE PLAYING POLICE INSPECTORS OR ARCHBISHOPS, THEY WERE WEARING THE SAME SHOES AS THEY HAD IN THE STREET.

TO THIS DAY, SHE NUMBERS MY SUCCESS BY THE PAIRS OF SHOES I HAVE LINED UP UNDER MY BED.

LINDSAY KEMP 1975

Lindsay with his Mum
Regent Street Theatre.
London 1974

MY FAMILY ALWAYS KNEW I WAS NEVER VERY INTERESTED IN FARMING BECAUSE, AT THE DROP OF A HAT, I'D BE OFF THAT TRACTOR, INTO THE HOUSE AND SKETCHING.

BILL GIBB 1974

Bill Gibb Fashion Show
Spring 1975

Asha Puthli
London 1974

David Haughton in costume in his role as the angel
On the set of 'Flowers'.
Fashion shoot with Birgit Underwood
(Wife of George, long-time Bowie friend).
Clothes by Bill Gibb.
Bush Theatre, London 1974

Bill Gibb
'High Glam' Fashion designer, close friend of Mick Rock. 1975

Bill Gibb fashion show
Spring 1975

Album cover shoot for Asha Puthli
Jazz singer. Make-up by Pierre Laroche. Clothes by Bill Gibb, 1974

Steve Harley
Cockney Rebel's leader. Clothes specially designed for Steve by Bill Gibb. Steve was (and is) a great talent, with a generous heart, a lyricist who ranks with the best. A performer of passion. 'Come up and see me', anytime.
London 1975

THE FIRST TIME I SAW ZIGGY STARDUST IT BOWLED ME OVER.
I WAS A JOURNALIST AT THE TIME, BUT THAT'S WHEN I DECIDED
I WANTED TO WRITE SONGS AND PERFORM.

TO BE HONEST, THE MAKE-UP AND CLOTHES HAVE ALWAYS
BEEN A WAY TO ATTRACT ATTENTION. IMAGE IS OBVIOUSLY
IMPORTANT AND I'M PREPARED TO DO WHATEVER IT TAKES.
BUT IT'S JUST A WAY OF GETTING PEOPLE TO LISTEN
TO THE MUSIC.

STEVE HARLEY 1974

MICK RONSON WAS ENORMOUSLY TALENTED, AND WHAT THE TWO OF THEM DID TOGETHER! OBVIOUSLY DAVID WAS THE DRIVING FORCE BUT MICK, YOU KNOW, MICK WAS THE PERFECT FOIL.

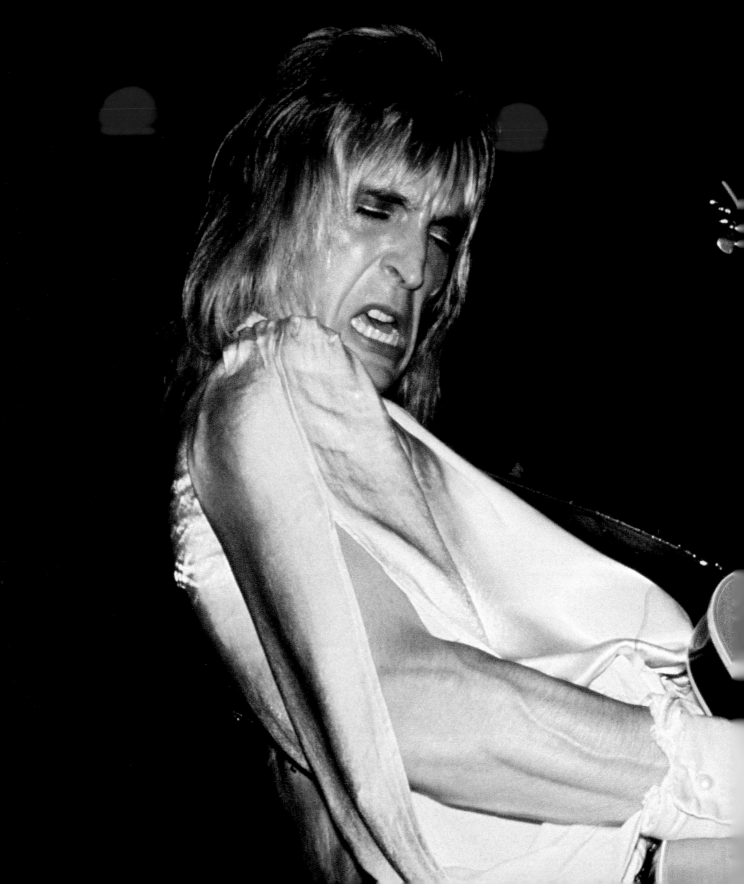

MICK WAS THE MASCULINE FORCE. WHEN THE TWO OF THEM GOT TOGETHER YOU CAN SEE DAVID'S ON HIS KNEES! DAVID'S PLAYING THE GIRL, NOT MICK.

MICK ROCK 1994

ude '72

he original cover photo for Mott The Hoople's classic Bowie-produced album All The Young Dudes' (David also wrote he song - one of Glam's foremost nthems). Why it wasn't used I can't emember, nor can Ian Hunter, must have een a chemical shift.

Camden Town, Summer 1972

Mott The Hoople
Rainbow Theatre 1974

Mick Ronson and Ian Hunter
Dorchester Hotel, London 1975

Ian Hunter
Bournemouth 1972

Mott The Hoople
Southend 1972

Overend Watts
1972

David and Lou
Bowie press junket. Dorchester Hotel.
London, Summer 1972

David with Freddie Burutti
His friend and personal clothing designer.
Scotland 1973

Lou
Suit by Freddie Burutti.
Wimbledon 1972

WHEN I SHOWED LOU THE CONTACT SHEETS, HE ZEROED
IN ON THE TRANSFORMER SHOT. I MADE THE PRINT
MYSELF - AS I USUALLY DID THOSE DAYS.
   THE FIRST TEST I MADE FELL OUT OF FOCUS IN THE
EXPOSURE. LOU LOVED THE RESULT. IT TOOK ME TWELVE
ATTEMPTS TO REPRODUCE THIS ACCIDENT FOR THE FINAL
LARGER PRINT FOR THE ALBUM COVER.

   MICK ROCK 1995

I ALWAYS LOVED LOU. I THOUGHT HE WAS FABULOUS
IN ALL WAYS AND THE FACT THAT HE WAS A COMPLETELY
FUCKED UP IMPERFECT HUMAN BEING, WELL, THAT
NEVER WORRIED ME. TO ME, THAT WAS THE SIGN OF
A TRUE ARTIST. I ALWAYS SAW THE DARK AND THE
LIGHT WITH LOU.

MICK ROCK 1986

Lou Reed
Blake's Hotel.
London. Summer 1975

Lou Reed
In his blonde period.
London 1974

BLONDE IS JUST A STATE OF MIND.
YOU DEFINITELY HAVE MORE FUN. I'VE BEEN
SO POPULAR SINCE I DYED MY HAIR.

LOU REED 1974

David and Lou
At a benefit for 'Save the Whales'.
Lou came on stage to perform 'White
Light White Heat' with David, the first
time he had ever appeared before an
English audience.
Royal Festival Hall, Summer 1972

NOBODY HAS EVER BEEN ABLE TO PUT THEIR FINGER ON ME
BECAUSE I'M NOT REALLY HERE. AT LEAST NOT THE WAY
THEY THINK I AM. IT'S ALL IN THEIR HEADS.
WHAT I'M INTO IS MINDLESSNESS. I JUST EMPTY MYSELF OUT,
SO WHAT PEOPLE SEE IS JUST A PROJECTION OF THEIR OWN
NEEDS. I DON'T DO OR SAY ANYTHING.

LOU REED 1975

Artists Kevin Whitney and Luciana Martinez
*Mainstays of the London 'Glam' social
scene. Biba's New Year party.*
London 1974/75

Amanda Lear
*Transsexual glam icon, muse to
Salvador Dali and here compere for Bowie
of his '1980 Floor Show' at the Marquee.*
November 1973

Syd Barrett
Earl's Court 1969

Cockney Rebel
*From the session for the album cover
'The Psychomodo'.*
London 1974

David Johansson of the New York Dolls
Biba's Rainbow Room.
1974

Debbie Harry
NYC, November 1977

The Dead Boys
*America's notorious answer to the
Sex Pistols (heavy on attitude), from
the album cover session for
'We have Come For Your Children'.*
Miami, January 1978

Nico, Eno, Kevin Ayers, John Cale
A shot for their 'June 1974' album cover.

The Pointer Sisters
*Backstage, just before their first ever UK
concert, Palladium Theatre, London.
Make-up by Pierre Laroche.*

Roxy Music
Post-Eno.
London 1975

Cockney Rebel
My first ever session with them.
London, December 1973

Blondie
The most commercially successful act
to arise from CBGB's in the
New York Punk scene.
But Debbie Harry was also totally Glam.
NYC, Spring 1978

Iggy and the Stooges
A ferocious chemically riddled band,
totally Glam but also the first and finest
ever punk band.
London, Summer 1972

Raw Power
Shot at King's Cross Theatre during Iggy and the Stooges one and only English concert. It only lasted forty minutes but to this day it remains the stuff of legend. Awesome and anarchic, the inspiration for all the punk bands of the mid and late seventies.
London, Summer 1972

ALL THE STOOGES WERE PRETTY WHACKED OUT. THEY WERE THE FIRST TO ADMIT IT. I'VE HEARD IGGY SAY THAT WHEN HE GOT BACK TO THE STATES AFTER THE 'RAW POWER' SESSIONS, HE COULD HARDLY STAND UP. HE'S JUST LUCKY HE'S PHYSICALLY STRONG. OR MAYBE HE'S JUST LUCKY... FOR A LITTLE GUY HE HAS AN AMAZING CONSTITUTION.

I MEAN HIM AND LOU, WHAT THEY PUT THEIR NERVOUS SYSTEMS THROUGH... I RAN PRETTY HARD MYSELF, BUT I WAS AN AMATEUR COMPARED TO THOSE TWO.

MICK ROCK 1976

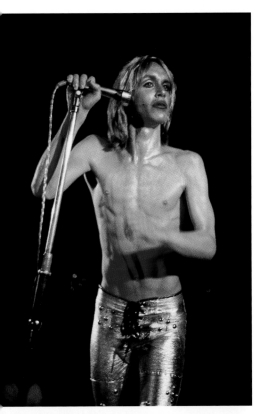
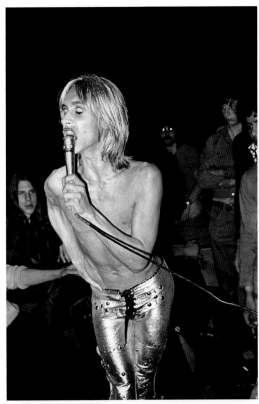

THERE'S NOTHIN' TO TELL, REALLY. JUST LISTEN TO THE MUSIC.
Y'SEE I'M NOT INTO ANYTHIN' REALLY. LET'S PUT IT LIKE THIS.
WHAT I'M INTO I'D NEVER TELL. I'D NEVER TELL MY REAL
FEELINGS ABOUT PEOPLE, THINGS, SITUATIONS.
FUCK NO. THAT'S MY BUSINESS. NO WAY. I'M REALLY A
VERY PRIVATE KIND OF GUY.

IGGY POP 1972

WHEN A COLLECTIVE AUDIENCE LIKE THIS WAS CONFRONTED
WITH IGGY POP - THE AUTHENTIC EMBODIMENT OF THEIR
WORST FEARS - THEY SCRAMBLED PHILOSOPHICALLY FOR
COVER. HE HAD ALREADY TRADED IN ALIENATION AND DESPAIR
FOR THE MORE AGGRESSIVE VERSION; NIHILISM.

MICK ROCK 1972

ROCK'N'ROLL IS SOMETIMES MORE THAN JUST MUSIC AND STARS. IN THE EARLY SEVENTIES LOU REED, DAVID BOWIE AND IGGY POP SYNTHESIZED AND REFLECTED NOT ONLY THE FURTHER REACHES OF POPULAR MUSIC, BUT ALSO OF LIFESTYLES IN GENERAL. THEY WERE SENSIBILITY PURVEYORS.

MICK ROCK 1990

WHAT'S MOST INTERESTING ABOUT
THOSE THREE - THE UNHOLY TRINITY -
BESIDES THE AMAZING CAREERS THEY ALL
HAVE - IS THE FACT THAT THEY ARE
STILL ALIVE.

MICK ROCK 1996

David, Iggy and Lou
Tea time at the Dorchester Hotel.
London, Summer 1972

Lou, Mick and David
The infamous 'Ziggy Stardust Farewell Party'.
Café Royal, London, July 1973

Lou, Mick and David
The infamous 'Ziggy Stardust Farewell Party'.
Café Royal, London, July 1973

Iggy, Angie Bowie, Sue Fussey (Bowie's hairdresser and wardrobe mistress), Spider and bass player Trevor Boulder and Lou
Dorchester Hotel, Summer 1972

Lou, Mick, Lulu, David, Geoff MacCormack (Bowie backing vocalist and long-time friend) and drummer Aynsley Dunbar
Café Royal 1973

IT WAS A TALE OF TWO CITIES. LONDON AND NEW YORK. I USED TO POP BACK AND FORTH BETWEEN THE TWO. THEY TUMBLED INTO EACH OTHER. THE WARHOL SCENE IN NEW YORK FED INTO THE GLAM SCENE IN LONDON. THERE WAS THIS CARNIVOROUS INTERCHANGE GOING ON BETWEEN THE TWO FACTIONS. IT WAS VERY ARTY, GLIB AND BISEXUAL.

MICK ROCK 1992

Mick Rock
Photo by Lou Reed. This was taken as
the sun came up after an all-night
session with Lou.
Balcony at Blake's Hotel, London 1974

Luciana Martinez
Artist. Biba's New Year Party.
London 1974/75

Ronnie Spector
Biba's Rainbow Room.
London 1974

ANDREW LOGAN IS FAMOUS AMONG THE FAMOUS FOR CERTAIN UNIQUE EVENTS HE STAGES. MOST RENOWNED OF ALL IS HIS OWN SPECIAL BRAND OF 'MISS WORLD' CONTEST, A YEARLY EVENT WHERE WOMEN AND MEN COMPETE ON EQUAL TERMS. IN 1974, 500 OF LONDON'S BRIGHTEST AND MOST BEAUTIFUL CRAMMED THEMSELVES INTO THE MUSTY, OLD WAREHOUSE ANDREW USES AS A STUDIO. ACTORS, MUSICIANS, ARTISTS, MODELS, PHOTOGRAPHERS WERE ALL THERE.

SOME 30 OR SO CONTESTANTS TROD THE STAGE, WHICH WAS DECORATED IN TYPICAL LOGAN FASHION WITH PIECES OF HIS WORK AND JUNK SHOP REJECTS. ANDREW HAD HOPED THAT A WOMAN MIGHT CLAIM THE CROWN, BUT THE WINNER TURNED OUT TO BE FILM-MAKER, DEREK JARMAN.

MICK ROCK 1975

First ever 'Alternative Miss World' winner cabaret performer Eric Roberts, crowns his successor Derek Jarman (set designer and underground film-maker)
Autumn 1974

Andrew Logan at home
Glam artist, sculptor and party-giver.
Camden Town, London 1974

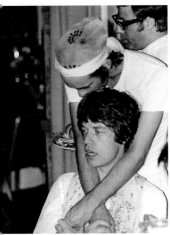

Left to right:
Mick Jagger and friend
David Johansson
Andrew Logan and Barbara Hulanicki

Andrew Logan and friends
Andrew is sporting his favourite party
outfit/dress suit left, evening dress right.
Boy meets girl glam style.
London 1975

MOST OF THE CLOTHES I WEAR COME FROM JUMBLE SALES,
SOME DISTRICTS I'VE LEARNED ARE MORE FRUITFUL THAN
OTHERS. WIMBLEDON IS VERY GOOD. SO IS BARNES. AND
JEWISH JUMBLE SALES IN HACKNEY ON SUNDAY MORNINGS.
LIFE FOR ME IS AN ETERNAL JUMBLE SALE.
ANDREW LOGAN 1975

Biba's
New Year Party.
1974/75

Bryan Ferry and Amanda Lear
Biba's Rainbow Room.
1974

Roxy Music
London 1975

Bryan Ferry
*Bryan Ferry was the only rocker of this
period to challenge David Bowie's
sartorial pre-eminence.*
Holland Park, London 1975

Bryan Ferry

Brian Eno

Eno and Roxy saxophonist Andy Mackay

All photos taken at the Rainbow Theatre, Roxy's first high-profile concert on the release of ther first album. They were the support act for Bowie's Lindsay Kemp staged performance.
Finsbury Park, London, August 1972

THERE'S A TENDENCY
TOWARDS GLAMORISATION IN
MY PHOTOS. BUT IT'S
A VERY PARTICULAR MIX OF
GLAMOUR. BAUDELAIRE
MEETS GEORGE HURRELL.
MAD POETS AND MOVIE
STARS. BOHEMIANISM MEETS
HIGH GLAM.

MICK ROCK 1978

Bryan Ferry performing in full tuxedo
Royal Albert Hall, London 1976

Headlining the Rainbow Theatre
Finsbury Park, London 1975

ABOVE ALL, ROXY MUSIC IS A STATE OF MIND.
HOLLYWOOD MOVIES MEETS ENGLISH ART SCHOOL,
WITH A LITTLE SCHOPENHAUER THROWN IN,
BOTH IN THE LYRICS I WRITE AND THE WAY WE
LOOK. OF COURSE, THAT ALLOWS FOR ALL KINDS
OF POSSIBILITIES. I AM, YOU MIGHT SAY,
A COLLAGISTE.
BRYAN FERRY 1975

Bryan Ferry at home
In his 'Our Man in Havana' period.
He was living with Jerry Hall at the time.
Holland Park, London 1976

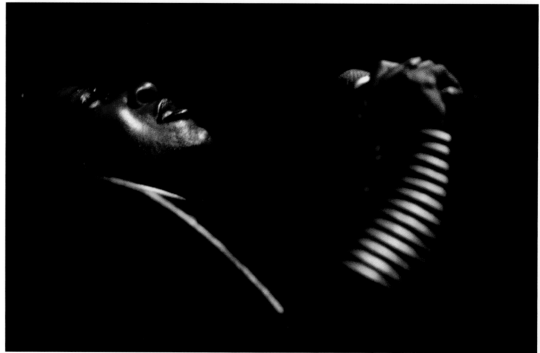

Bryan Ferry
Royal Albert Hall, London 1976

Patti Labelle
Drury Lane Theatre, London 1974

Patti Smith
Princess of Punk.
N.Y.C, Autumn 1976

Bowie
Costume by Kansai, make-up by Pierre Laroche.
Hammersmith Odeon, London, Summer 1973

Iggy Pop
London 1972

Mick Jagger
Earl's Court, London 1975

Steve Harley
UK 1975

David Johansson
Mercer Arts Centre, NYC, September 1972

YOU SEE, AN ARTIST'S MOTIVES DON'T MATTER AT ALL. I MEAN NOT ONE ARTIST, ONE SONG HAS EVER CHANGED THIS WORLD.

THE ARTIST DOESN'T EXIST.
HE'S STRICTLY A FIGMENT OF THE PUBLIC'S IMAGINATION.

NONE OF US EXIST.
WE'RE IN THE TWILIGHT ZONE.
WE'LL ALL GO TO HELL, 'CAUSE WE
SET OURSELVES UP AS GODS.

DAVID BOWIE 1972

THEY'RE ALL VERY EDUCATED. TWO OF THEM HAVE PHD'S;
ROGER TAYLOR IS TRAINED TO BE A DENTIST.
THEY WERE NEVER WORKING CLASS LADS.

MICK ROCK 1975

My first studio session with Queen
Great Newport Street, London,
December 1973

The 'nude' session
*This rattled the cages of a few less
adventurous rock critics. But it certainly
gave Queen the attention they wanted.*

NATURAL TO ME. I'M A DANDY, A SHOWOFF. I GET VERY HIGH
ON ALL THE ATTENTION. I LOVE IT.

FREDDIE MERCURY 1974

From the 'Queen II'
inner sleeve session.

From the 'Sheer Heart Attack' album cover session
For a moment, this was an early front runner for the cover.
Summer 1974

QUEEN WILL ALWAYS CARRY ON IN OUR SAME EXTREME, CRAZY, CONFIDENT MANNER. I MEAN, WHAT WE PROJECT IS AN ORIGINAL SOUND AND PRESENTATION WORKED UP TO PERFECT QUALITY. WE DON'T DO ANYTHING BY HALF MEASURES. EITHER IT'S THE BEST OR WE DON'T BOTHER. COMPROMISE IS NOT A WORD WE UNDERSTAND. WE KNOW WHAT WE WANT AND NEED AND NO ONE COULD EVER PERSUADE US DIFFERENTLY. WE'LL ALWAYS ARGUE CONSTANTLY AMONGST OURSELVES ABOUT HOW THINGS SHOULD BE DONE. AND WE'LL ALWAYS GIVE OUR BEST.

FREDDIE MERCURY 1974

Andrew Logan
London 1975

MY LIES ARE SIMPLY ECSTATIC EXAGGERATIONS.
LINDSAY KEMP 1974

The Cycle Sluts
*San Fransisco's infamous theatre group, who
fetchingly sported beards with their drag.*
London 1975

**Patrick Cargill (actor), Larry Parnes
(producer of 'Flowers' and The Cycle Sluts),
Lindsay Kemp, Danny La Rue, Peter Wyngarde (actor)**
After the opening of 'Flowers'.
Backstage at the Regent Theatre, London 1975

FAIRY ROSES, FAIRY RINGS,
TURN OUT SOMETIMES TROUBLESOME THINGS.

W.M. THACKERAY 1855

A GAY PERSON GETS A COMPLETELY DIFFERENT
SET OF REACTIONS TO WHAT A STRAIGHT HETERO
GETS. MUCH STRONGER ONES. WHEN I ENFORCE
MY ROLE AS BISEXUAL OF THE EVENING,
EVERYONE DOES THEIR LITTLE ACT. SOME OF IT'S
A SHOW THING. TO GET OTHER PEOPLE GOING.
A LOT OF GAY PEOPLE ARE VERY INSECURE AND
HAVE TO ASSERT THEMSELVES. BUT JUST LIKE
THERE'S ALL KINDS OF STRAIGHTS, SO THERE'S
ALL KINDS OF GAY. THEY'RE PEOPLE, INDIVIDUALS.
THAT'S WHAT'S IMPORTANT.

DAVID BOWIE 1973

Gustavo
Famed Brazilian drag queen.
London 1975

FRANK'N'FURTER IS REALLY SUCH A BIZARRE
CHARACTER; SUCH A STRONG, CRAZY
CHARACTER. HE HAS A VERY ODD APPEAL,
PARTICULARLY TO WOMEN. HE'S JUST ANOTHER
VARIATION OF THE MAD SCIENTIST REALLY,
AND HE IS FUNNY. THE ODD THING ABOUT
FRANK IS THAT HE CAN GO FROM DOING
SOMETHING REALLY OUTRAGEOUS AND
HORRIFIC, TO BEING DEEPLY ENDEARING,
SORT OF JOLLY.

TIM CURRY 1975

Tim Curry as Frank'n'Furter
On the set of 'Rocky Horror Picture Show'
Bray Studios, Autumn 1974

Susan Sarandon as Janet

Peter Hinwood, Little Nell, Tim Curry,
Susan Sarandon and Barry Bostwick

FRANK IS NO MORE CORRUPTING THAN A PANTOMIME DAME. HE'S SO TOTALLY INDIVIDUAL, A FUN CHARACTER. HE'S A BIG BLOKE IN DRAG, AND NOT EVEN IN DRAG REALLY. MORE IN UNDERWEAR. FRANK IS ABSURDLY MASCULINE.

TIM CURRY 1975

Mick Rock
Doing his best Tim Curry impersonation.
Autumn 1974

I WROTE 'ROCKY HORROR'
FOR MYSELF. I JUST PUT
TOGETHER ALL THE THINGS I
LIKE: SCIENCE FICTION, OLD
MOVIES, COMICS, DRAG,
ROCK'N'ROLL. IT'S JUST A BIT
OF MAKE-BELIEVE WITH A
FEW SONGS.

RICHARD O'BRIEN 1975

Richard O'Brien
*(Rocky Horror's author) as Riff Raff,
Frank's man servant.*

Little Nell as Columbia, Pat Quinn as
Magenta with Frank

Little Nell

Noddy Holder of Slade
Earl's Court, 1973

Dave Hill of Slade
Earl's Court, 1973

Brian Connelly of The Sweet
Rainbow Theatre, 1973

Steve Priest of the Sweet
Rainbow Theatre, 1973

Alice Cooper
'Schools Out' Tour.
Wembley, London 1974

Arthur Brown and Kingdom Come
London 1974

Patti Labelle
Drury Lane Theatre.
London 1974

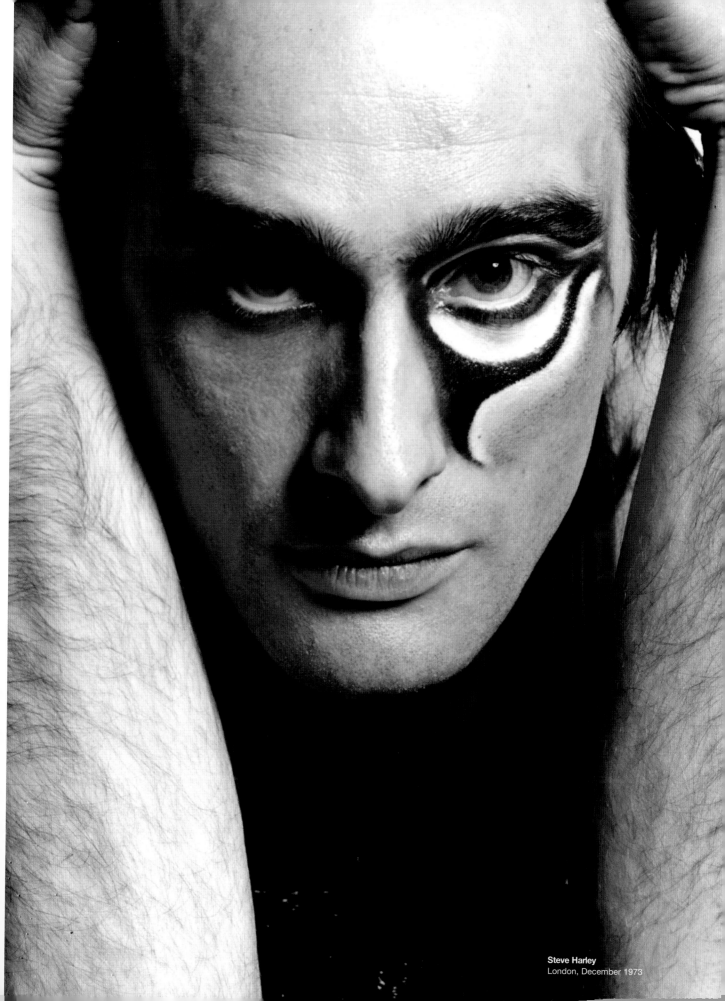

Steve Harley
London, December 1973

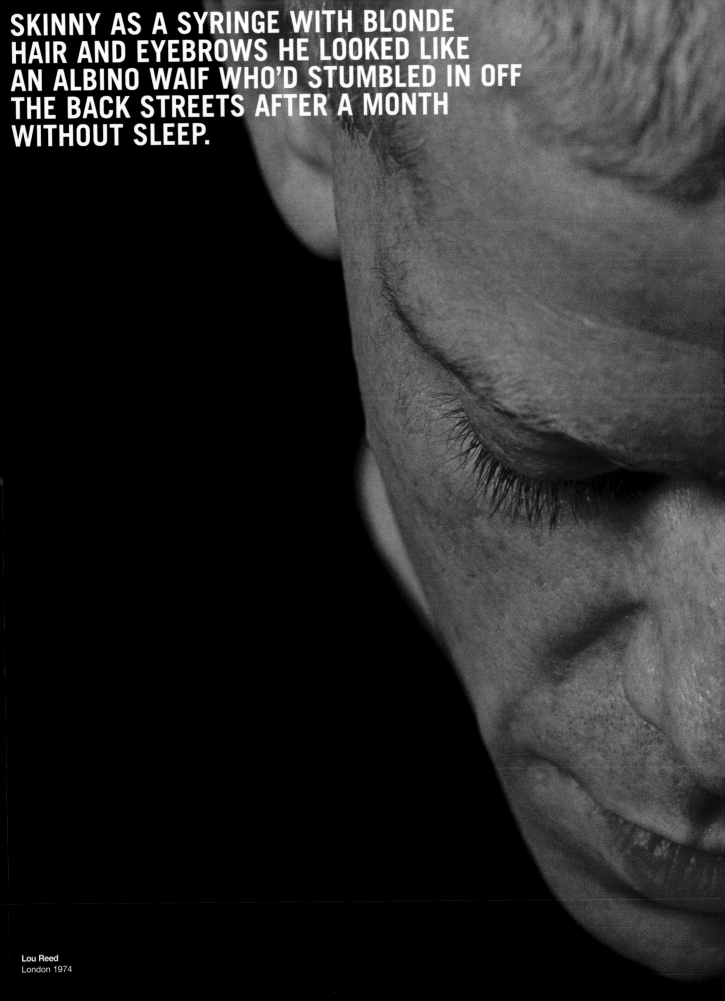

SKINNY AS A SYRINGE WITH BLONDE
HAIR AND EYEBROWS HE LOOKED LIKE
AN ALBINO WAIF WHO'D STUMBLED IN OFF
THE BACK STREETS AFTER A MONTH
WITHOUT SLEEP.

Lou Reed
London 1974

HE LOOKED LOST AND
OUT OF PLACE IN THE
DAYLIGHT, CREATURE OF
GLOOM AND NIGHT.

MICK ROCK ON
LOU REED 1974

Cyrinda Foxe and Angie Bowie
After Bowie's first ever New York concert
at Carnegie Hall.
Plaza Hotel, September 1972

Angie Bowie
Haddon Hall, Beckenham 1973

Angie and Dana Gillespie
Singer and one-time girlfriend of Bowie,
'Ziggy Farewell party'. 1973

Ian Hunter
Mott The Hoople's frontman. A great songwriter with a classic rock'n'roll image.
London 1977

Daniella
Model and babysitter for the Bowies' and girlfriend of Freddie Burutti.
London 1973

Mick Ronson
Sans make-up.
Bournemouth 1973

Amanda Lear
London 1974

ONCE I WENT BLONDE, THERE WAS NO TURNING BACK. AND WHEN
THE ROOTS BEGAN TO SHOW, I JUST GOT TOO LAZY TO DEAL WITH IT,
AND PEOPLE LOVED IT EVEN MORE.

DEBBIE HARRY 1977

Debbie Harry
She had just cut her hair, so she didn't look as perfectly trashy Glam as usual. But the short cut suited her (as you can see).
NYC 1978

Marianne Faithful
At the Marquee for Bowie's final Ziggy performance for American TV's, 'Midnight Special' entitled 'The 1980 Floor Show'.
November 1973

I KNOW THAT ONE DAY A BIG ARTIST IS
GOING TO GET KILLED ON STAGE, AND I
KNOW THAT WE'RE GOING TO GO VERY BIG.
AND I KEEP THINKING: IT'S BOUND TO BE
ME. GO OUT ON ME FIRST TOUR, GET DONE
IN AT ME FIRST GIG, AN' NOBODY WILL
EVER SEE ME. THAT WOULD
MAKE ME WILD.

DAVID BOWIE 1974

Marianne and Bowie
*The nun's oufit played exquisitely against
her image of rock tart/ doper. She certainly
looked very angelic.*
The Marquee, London 1973

FOR THE SAKE OF GETTING AWAY FROM THE STRAITJACKET OF AN IMAGE, I SHALL CONTRADICT MYSELF. I CAN'T AFFORD TO BE ONE THING ALL THE TIME. I'D DIE. I LOVE THE CHANGE. IF NECESSARY, I SHALL JUST LIE A LOT.

Bowie
Beverly Hills Hotel.
October 1972.

I THINK I SHALL SET UP A WHOLE TRAIL OF LIES. THAT'S A GOOD IDEA. THAT WOULD GIVE ME A LOT OF SCOPE. THAT'S WHAT CREATES THE MYTH IN THE PUBLIC EYE.

DAVID BOWIE 1973

Spiders in the USA
1972

Spiders in the UK
1973

'Jean Genie' promo film
San Francisco, November 1972

Mick Rock and Bowie make classic promo art
San Francisco, 1972

LIKE A BEAUTIFUL MARIONETTE HE WAVES HIS LONG LEGS AND
ROLLS HIS WELL-OILED HIPS. IF HE'S A TART, AS HE'S OFTEN
DESCRIBED HIMSELF, HE'S UNDOUBTEDLY HIGH-CLASS. HIS
MAKE-UP IS PERFECT, HIS STAGE CLOTHES ARE SEDUCTIVELY
FLAMBOYANT AND BEAUTIFULLY FITTED, AND ...

HE DOESN'T SWEAT. HE ROCKS AND SWINGS THROUGH A WHOLE
NINETY-MINUTE SET WITHOUT A GLIMMER. NEITHER IS HE JUST A
TEASE, AS WE ALL SOON DISCOVER. HE MIGHT POUT, TILT HIS HEA
COQUETTISHLY, GIGGLE, BUT HE COMES UP WITH THE GOODS.

MICK ROCK 1972

Holding original 'Hunky Dory' cover art
Beckenham, March 1972

I'M A TIGHTROPE WALKER. ALWAYS HAVE BEEN. THAT'S THE ONLY WAY I KNOW HOW TO LIVE.
DAVID BOWIE 1973

Artwork by the author, costume by Kansai

NORMALLY BEFORE A BATTLE THE MEN WOULD
MAKE THEMSELVES UP TO LOOK AS BEAUTIFUL AND
AMAZING AS POSSIBLE. THEN THEY'D GO OUT
AND HACK EACH OTHER TO PIECES. THAT'S NOT MY
BAG, OF COURSE. BUT BASED ON THAT YOU CAN
HARDLY CALL MAKE-UP UNMASCULINE.
AND LOOK AT ALL THE OLD KINGS AND DANDIES.

AND IF YOU LOOK TO THE ANIMAL WORLD, SO OFTEN
THE MALE IS MORE BEAUTIFUL THAN THE FEMALE -
LOOK AT PEACOCKS AND LIONS.

REALLY MAKE-UP AND BEAUTIFUL CLOTHES ARE
FUNDAMENTAL TO ME. IT'S JUST THAT WE LIVE IN
SUCH A STRANGE SOCIETY.

DAVID BOWIE 1972

TIRED OF ARTIFICIAL FLOWERS APEING REAL ONES,
HE WANTED SOME NATURAL FLOWERS THAT
WOULD LOOK LIKE FAKES.

JORIS-KARL HUYSMANS, *À REBOURS*, 1884

Bee Mine
1979

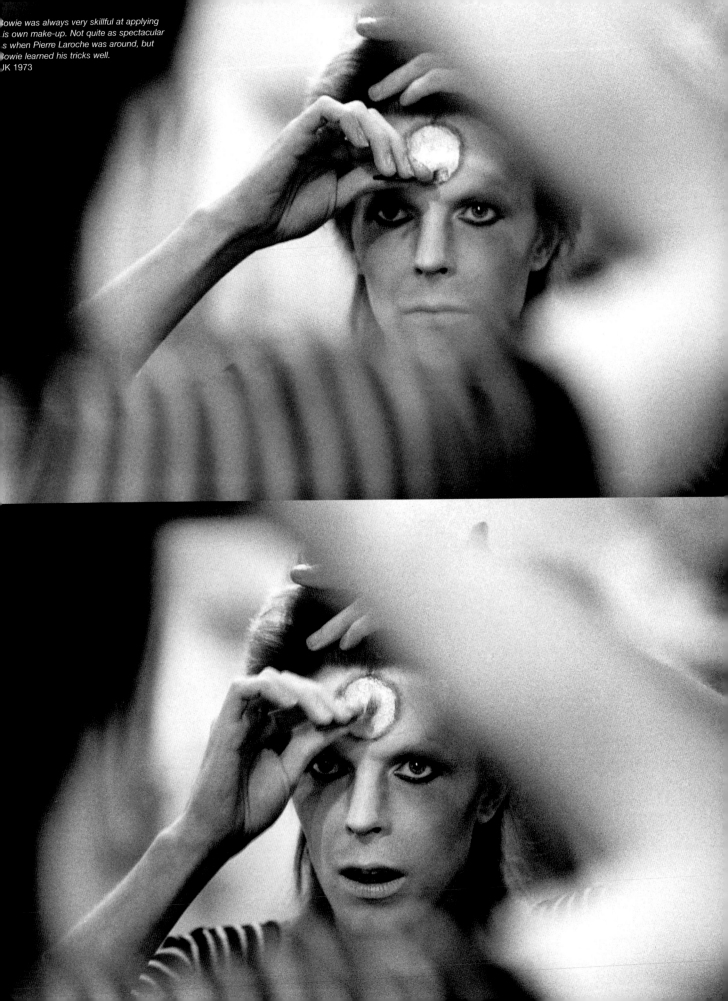

Bowie was always very skillful at applying his own make-up. Not quite as spectacular as when Pierre Laroche was around, but Bowie learned his tricks well.
UK 1973

At the hotel where he changed for the show.
The photo bottom right was the cover of
'Rolling Stone', 9 November 1972.
Chicago, 2 October 1972

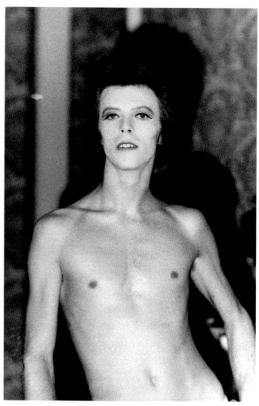

MY WHOLE LIFE SWINGS FROM HIGH CLASS TO LOW. I'M A REAL CULTURE VULTURE. EVERYBODY'S VULTURE I AM. I LIVE OFF THE WORLD. I THINK I MAKE GOOD USE OF IT, I TELL YER. I'LL TAKE EVERYTHING IT'S GOT.

DAVID BOWIE 1972

Freddie Mercury
Mixing 'Night at the Opera.'
London 1975

FREDDIE'S TEETH WERE HIS PRIME CONCERN
WHEN TAKING PHOTOS. THEY TENDED TO PROTRUDE
AND HE WANTED TO DISGUISE THIS. ONE DAY HE
OPENED HIS MOUTH WIDE TO SHOW ME THE
PROBLEM. HE HAD TOO MANY TEETH. FOUR EXTRA
AT THE BACK OF HIS PALATE WHICH PUSHED THE
OTHERS FORWARD.

WHEN I POINTED OUT THAT THIS WAS A RELATIVELY
EASY, IF PAINFUL, THING TO CORRECT, HE TOLD ME
HE COULDN'T. "I'M FRIGHTENED IT WILL AFFECT
MY VOICE. I NEED THE EXTRA TEETH." I NEVER
REALLY UNDERSTOOD WHY, BUT FREDDIE
WAS CONVINCED.

MICK ROCK 1992

Costume by Zandra Rhodes,
Queen's favourite designer.
London, Summer 1974

AT THE TIME WE FIRST DECIDED TO CALL OURSELVES
'QUEEN' IT WAS A VERY DIFFERENT NAME. PARTLY IT WAS
A REGAL THING, PARTLY CAMP. BUT THEN OF COURSE
THE WORD HADN'T COME INTO SUCH PROMINENCE.
TRY TELLING THAT TO PEOPLE NOWADAYS.

FREDDIE MERCURY 1975

I REMEMBER FREDDIE TELLING ME, "THE MOST IMPORTANT THING IS TO LIVE A FABULOUS LIFE. AS LONG AS IT'S FABULOUS, I DON'T CARE HOW LONG IT IS." FREDDIE MERCURY WAS ONE OF MY FAVOURITE HUMAN BEINGS, A GEM OF A MAN.
MICK ROCK 1995

Freddie and Mary Austin
Who he met managing the make-up section at Biba's. She was his girlfriend until he 'came out' and looked after him in his sad final years. He often said how he trusted her more than anyone he had ever known. Backstage, Rainbow Theatre
London 1974

Freddie with the author
Partying in 1974.

Freddie and Brian May
At Sarm Studios, mixing 'Night at the Opera'.
London 1975

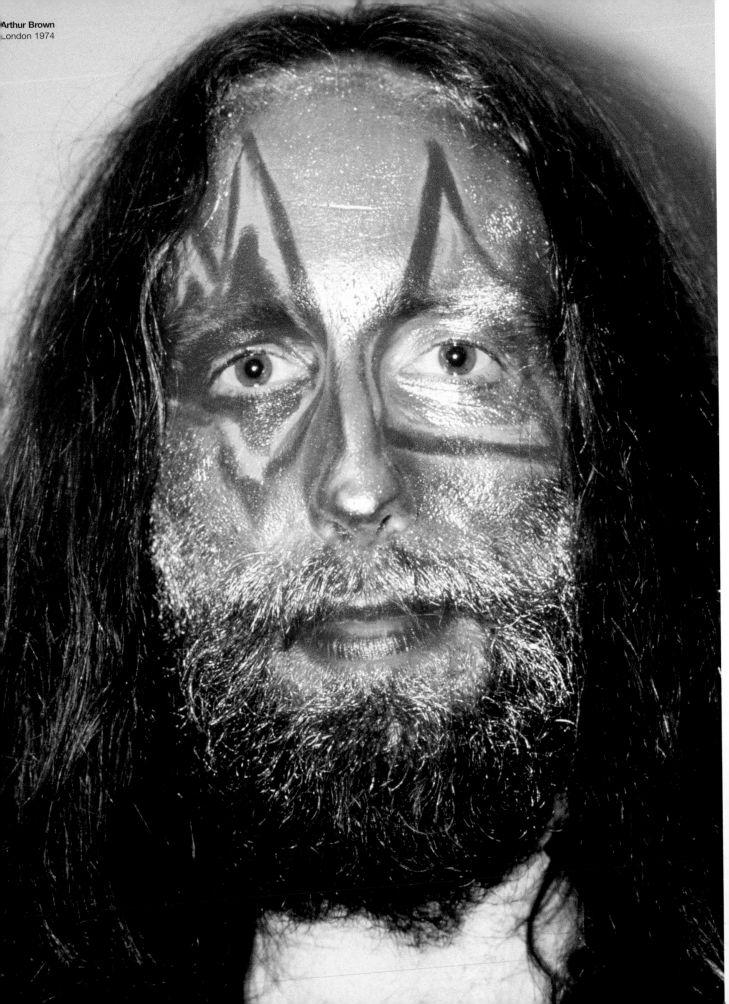

Lou and David
Café Royal, London 1973

Handbag
1975

**Mainstay of Lindsay Kemp troupe,
Blind Orlando and Celestino Coronado
(Documentary film maker)**
London 1974

Lindsay with Long John Baldry
Again, he was big on kissing!
1975

Lou with Judy Nylon
Café Royal, London 1973

Bianca Jagger and Angie Bowie
Café Royal, London 1975

**Lindsay (in Bill Gibb dress) and
David Haughton**
Bush theatre, London 1974

Andy Warhol and Lou Reed
'Rock'n'Roll Heart' end of tour party.
NYC, December 1976

Earl McGrath, Mick Jagger, Andy Warhol
Windows on the World.
NYC, December 1976

ANDY WARHOL ONCE SAID TO ME, YEARS AGO, THAT I WAS TO BE IN MUSIC, WHAT HE WAS TO THE VISUAL ARTS. YOU CAN'T DEFINE IT. BUT IT'S ALL HAPPENING THE WAY HE SAID IT WOULD. THE MAN'S AMAZING.

LOU REED 1974

Truman Capote and Andy Warhol
From a session at The Factory, Union Square, the Xmas issue of High Times magazine. Truman was smashed. Andy was philosophical. Note his pet Dachshund Archie, between them.
NYC 1979

LOU WAS A FASCINATING SUBJECT. HE HAD
AN ENIGMATIC PRESENCE; BUT WASN'T A VAIN MAN.
HE RARELY LOOKED IN THE MIRROR BUT WAS VERY
AWARE OF HIS VISUAL PERSONA. HE WAS NEVER
CRITICAL OF THE RESULTS OF A SESSION,
HE JUST ZONED IN ON WHAT HE LIKED AND
HE ESPECIALLY LIKED THIS FRAME.

MICK ROCK 1994

Lou Reed
Blake's Hotel, London 1975

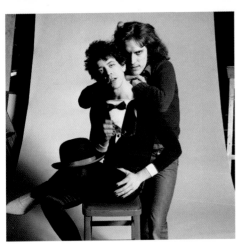

LOU REED HAS ALWAYS EPITOMISED NEW YORK FOR FELLOW ARTISTS AND MEDIA OBSERVERS, BOTH IN HIS LIFESTYLE AND HIS ART. THE CHRONICLER OF THE SHADOW WORLD, THE DEVIANTS, THE DRUG LIMBO, THE CONCRETE JUNGLE, HE IS THE POET LAUREATE OF THAT CITY. HIS NAME IS SYNONYMOUS WITH DECADENCE. YET HE HIMSELF LAYS NO CLAIM TO ANY OF THIS. "I JUST PUT THINGS OUT AND SIT AND WATCH." EVEN IN THE CITY OF ALIENATION, LOU LIVES IN HIS OWN LIMBO. "I PHONED UP THE DRUGSTORE JUST ROUND THE CORNER FROM WHERE I LIVE AND ASKED THEM TO DELIVER TO ME. I GAVE THEM MY ADDRESS. THEY SAID IT WAS IMPOSSIBLE. IT DIDN'T EXIST. I DON'T EVEN KNOW WHERE I LIVE".

MICK ROCK 1972

I MET MICK JAGGER'S YOUNGER BROTHER, CHRIS, WHILE I WAS AT CAMBRIDGE. HE USED TO TAKE A BUNCH OF US ON THE WEEKENDS TO JAGGER'S PLACE. ONE DAY CHRIS CAME IN WITH BRIAN JONES' ADDRESS BOOK. HE SAID, "LOOK AT THIS, IT'S BRIAN WHO HAS ALL THE GIRLFRIENDS." WE CALLED A COUPLE OF THE GIRLS JUST TO SEE IF THEY'D COME OVER. THEY CAME OVER.

MICK ROCK 1992

Jagger
Madison Garden.
NYC 1978

Mick and Keith
Earl's Court 1975

Brian Eno
Rainbow Theatre.
August 1972

Wayne County
Mercer Arts Centre.
NYC, September 1972

John Cale
Drury Lane Theatre.
London 1974

Ian Hunter, Mott the Hoople
UK 1973

DAVID'S MUSIC IS THE THING. FINALLY THAT'S WHAT COUNTS AND THAT'S WHAT'S MOST IMPORTANT IN HIS LIFE. WHEN ALL THE ANALYSING IS OVER, ALL THE TALK OF INTELLECTUAL BRILLIANCE, WHY DOES IT WORK? "I DON'T KNOW. I WRITE VERY MUCH THROUGH INSTINCT. I'M NOT AN INTELLECTUAL. THEY COME TOGETHER, WORDS AND MUSIC. I PUT IT ALL DOWN IN A CERTAIN WAY JUST 'CAUSE IT FEELS RIGHT."

MICK ROCK 1972

NOBODY HAS CREATED SUCH A STIR AS MR. B,
OLE ALADDIN SANE HIMSELF, SINCE THE TURN OF THE
DECADE. HE'S THE MOST PROVOCATIVE FIGURE IN
MODERN MUSIC. LISTEN TO HIS RECORDS.
WATCH HIM PERFORM. READ WHAT THE PRESS HAVE
TO SAY ABOUT HIM. WHERE DOES THAT LEAVE YOU?
CONFUSED PROBABLY. AND INTRIGUED. ACTOR, POET,
CLOWN AND, OF COURSE, SONGWRITER.

NOW YOU SEE HIM. NOW YOU DON'T. ROLL UP, ROLL UP.
I GIVE YOU THE NEW WIZARD OF ROCK. WHAT HE HAS
OVER ALL THE OTHER ROCK SUPERSTARS IS SHEER
CLASS. HE IS ABLE TO GENERATE POWERFUL IMAGES,
TO PROMOTE A SENSE OF MYTH, LIKE NO OTHER
MODERN STAR.

MICK ROCK 1973

THE ZEITGEIST FINALLY SHIFTED ONCE AND FOR ALL IN DECEMBER 1975 WHEN THE SEX PISTOLS PERFORMED THEIR FIRST EVER CONCERT AT THE CHELSEA ARTS COLLEGE XMAS PARTY. JOHNNY ROTTEN, THE TRUE GHOST IN THE MACHINE, ADMINISTERED THE COUP DE GRACE WHEN HE OPENED THE SHOW WITH THE WELCOME: "FUCK OFF YOU BUNCH OF WANKERS." A NATURAL WIT, AND A MASTER OF IRONY, HE MAY NOT (AS HE INTONED) HAVE BEEN THE ANTICHRIST, BUT HE WAS CERTAINLY THE ANTI-ROCKER. (OR MAYBE HE WAS JUST SOMEONE'S AUNTIE!).

'PUNK' HAD BEEN PERCOLATING UNDER SINCE THE SPRING OF 1974, WHEN PATTI SMITH, THE RAMONES, BLONDIE AND TELEVISION SURFACED IN NEW YORK AT CBGB'S. LACK OF TECHNICAL EXPERTISE WAS PROFFERED AS A VIRTUE. A RAW, AGGRESSIVE, UNCOMPROMISING ATTITUDE WAS EVERYTHING. POWER CHORDS AND RECKLESS LYRICS TOLD THE STORY.

BUT JOHNNY SPELLED THE FINAL DEATH RATTLE OF 'GLAM' WITH HIS SNARLING, SPITTING, CONTEMPTUOUS DEMEANOUR. 'PUNK' TRASHED THE MASCARA AND SATIN. SAFETY PINS AND RIPPED T-SHIRTS WERE THE NEW CALL TO ARMS.

MICK ROCK 1990

LOOK AT THE HAIRCOLOUR. JOHNNY ROTTEN WAS BASICALLY ZIGGY STARDUST WITH A VERY BAD ATTITUDE. THEY BOTH LOVED TO GET PEOPLE AT IT.

MICK ROCK 1984

ZIGGY STARDUST HAD A MUTANT BASTARD OFFSPRING AND HIS NAME WAS JOHNNY ROTTEN.

DAVID BOWIE 1980

Glen Matlock, Johnny, Steve Jones
London, January 1976

Johnny Rotten
High Times magazine cover.
1977

David Bowie
1972

Sex Pistols Live
Johnny solo at the very first Pistols performance, Chelsea Arts College.
London, December 1975

The Ramones
'End of the Century' album cover session.
NYC 1979

Patti Smith
NYC 1976

DEBBIE HARRY WAS INDEED *THE MARILYN MONROE OF PUNK* (AS THE PRESS LIKED TO DUB HER). BUT AS 'PUNK' AS SHE WAS, SHE WAS ALSO AS 'GLAM' AS A GIRL COULD BE. AND SHE ALWAYS HAD A GREAT SENSE OF HUMOUR ABOUT ALL THE ATTENTION. SHE NEVER LET IT INHIBIT HER ABILITY TO GET DOWN WITH THE BOYS. SHE WAS (AND IS) A FACE FOR THE AGES. AND A PRETTY GOOD SINGER AND SONGWRITER AS A BONUS...

MICK ROCK 1984

THE ONLY WAY TO REALLY PREPARE FOR SESSIONS IS TO FIRST
BUILD YOUR INTERNAL FOCUS. YOU HAVE TO PREPARE LIKE A
FIGHTER, KNOW HOW TO DUCK AND WEAVE, WHEN TO ATTACK,
WHEN TO PLAY ROPE-A-DOPE.

MICK ROCK 1975

Medusa
NYC 1980

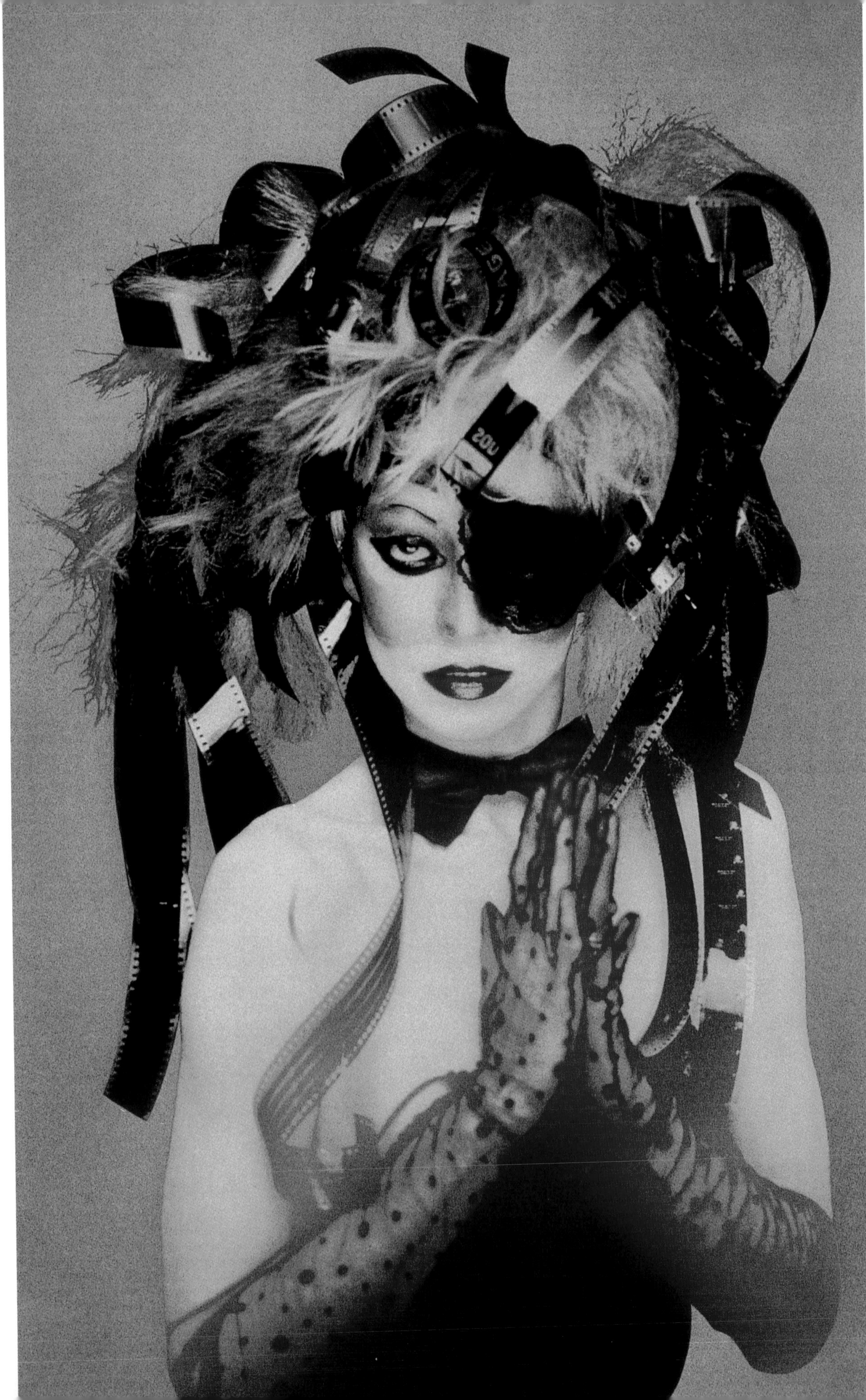

IF YOU WANT TO RULE THE WORLD, THERE IS ONLY ONE LAW: THE LAW OF COMPASSION AND THE SWEET TONGUE.

YOGI BHAJAN

FOR PATI AND NATHALIE, WHO KNOW THAT THERE IS NO GLITTER WITHOUT THE BLOOD...

Superbig thanks to:
David Bowie, a scholar (and a gentleman) and a rocker nonpareil
Paul West and Paula Benson, whose love of design shines through
Zoë Manzi, who edits with a fond intuition for all the madness
Sarah Marusek, for her patience and laughter
Steve Savigear and Emily Moore, who believe in the art of production
Alex Proud and Rankin, for their respect and enthusiasm
Daniel Abineri, who gave me the best of all titles

Special thanks also to:
Liz Vap, Joan Rock, Kirk, Dan, Suzanne, Diana, Briar, Ed and the rest
of the staff at Vision On; Hector Proud and the Idea Generation,
Alan Hamilton and Nina Scherer at Proud Galleries, Andy, Nick and all
the boys at AJD; Geraldine and Stefania at Sfera, Ginny Lohle and
all at Starfile, Catherine Alexander, Sat Jivan Kaur, Sat Jivan Singh,
Jacquie Rock-Meyer, Iris Keitel, Allen Klein, Andrew Loog Oldham,
Michael Chambers, John P. Serubo, Chris Murray of
Govinda Gallery, Richard Lasdon, Steve, Margaret and all at
N.Y. Filmworks; Aaron Trepanier, Rossi and staff at Milk Studios NYC,
and all the faces in this tome, without whom...

Strapps album cover
London 1976

Spike
NYC 1981

For Pati and Nathalie, my personal eyewitnesses to Nouveau Glam........

Super big thanks to:
David Bowie, a scholar (and a gentleman) and a rocker nonpareil
Chris Charlesworth, for his longtime support
Steve Wilson, for pushing the new agenda
Bob Wise, for keeping it all afloat
Paul West and Paula Benson, for their superb design layout
Alison Wofford, for first-rate publicity
Sarah Nesenjuk, for designing a great new cover
Liz Vap, for being a true believer
Andrew von Melchior, for his relentless enthusiasm
Annie Toglia, a soul sister who will never be forgotten

Special thanks also to: Pati and Nathalie, Iris Keitel, Allen Klein, Andrew Loog Oldham, Catherine Alexander, Dean Holtermann, Joan Rock, Richard Lasdon, Sat Jivan Kaur, Sat Jivan Singh, Shazi and Lucky of Digizone, NYC

This edition published 2013 by exclusive license by Omnibus Press
(A Division of Music Sales Limited)
ISBN: 978.1.780.38881.6
Order No: OP55165

Exclusive Distributors
Music Sales Limited
14-15 Berners Street, London W1T 3L J, UK.
Music Sales Corporation
180 Madison Avenue, 24th Floor, New York, NY 10016, USA.
Macmillan Distribution Services
53 Park West Drive, Derrimut, Vic 3030, Australia.

To the Music Trade only:
Music Sales Limited
14-15 Berners Street, London W1T 3L J, UK.

Printed in Singapore
A catalogue record for this book is available from the British Library.
Visit Omnibus Press on the web at www.omnibuspress.com
Prints of the photos included in this book can be purchased through www.mickrock.com

ROCK DREAMS

MICK ROCK BIBLIOGRAPHY:

MICK ROCK - A PHOTOGRAPHIC RECORD 1969-1980
CENTURY 22 BOOKS 1995

PSYCHEDELIC RENEGADES / SYD BARRETT
GENESIS PUBLICATIONS 2002

MOONAGE DAYDREAM/ZIGGY STARDUST
(WITH DAVID BOWIE)
GENESIS PUBLICATIONS 2002

ROCK 'N' ROLL EYE
TOKYO METROPOLITAN MUSEUM OF PHOTOGRAPHY
2003

KILLER QUEEN (WITH BRIAN MAY)
GENESIS PUBLICATIONS 2003

PICTURE THIS / DEBBIE HARRY AND BLONDIE
(WITH A FOREWORD BY DEBBIE HARRY)
SANCTUARY PUBLICATIONS 2004

RAW POWER / IGGY AND THE STOOGES
(WITH A FOREWORD BY IGGY POP)
OMNIBUS PRESS BOOKS 2005

ROCKY HORROR
(WITH A FOREWORD BY RICHARD O'BRIEN)
SCHWARZKOPF & SCHWARZKOPF 2006

TRANSFORMER (WITH LOU REED)
GENESIS PUBLICATIONS 2006